ON YOUR ANNIVERSARY

ON YOUR ANNIVERSARY

EDITED BY CATHERINE KOUTS AND LAURA CAVALUZZO
PHOTOGRAPHY BY ELISABETH FALL

GIBBS·SMITH
➔P
PUBLISHER

SALT LAKE CITY

First Edition
99 98 97 96   5 4 3 2 1

Photographs copyright © 1996 by Elisabeth Fall

This is a Peregrine Smith Book, published by
Gibbs Smith, Publisher
P.O. Box 667
Layton, UT 84041

Design by The Stiebling Group
In-house editing by Dawn Valentine Hadlock
Cover photograph by Elisabeth Fall

Library of Congress Cataloging-in-Publication Data

On your anniversary / edited by Catherine Kouts and Laura Cavaluzzo ;
    photography by Elisabeth Fall. — 1st ed.
          p.   cm.
      "This is a Peregrine Smith book"—T.p. verso.
      ISBN 0-87905-461-1
      1. Marriage —Quotations, maxims, etc.   I. Kouts, Catherine.
    II. Cavaluzzo, Laura.
    PN6084.M305   1996
306.81—dc20   96-16560
                                                                    CIP

Printed and bound in Singapore

To

From

On the occasion of your anniversary

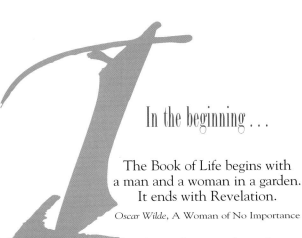

In the beginning . . .

The Book of Life begins with
a man and a woman in a garden.
It ends with Revelation.

Oscar Wilde, A Woman of No Importance

Oh, what a dear ravishing thing is
the beginning of an Amour!

Aphra Behn, The Emperor of the Moon

I was at a party feeling very shy because there were
a lot of celebrities around, and I was sitting in a corner
alone and a very beautiful young man came up to me and
offered me some salted peanuts and he said,
"I wish they were emeralds" as he handed me the peanuts
and that was the end of my heart. I never got it back.

Helen Hayes, in an interview with a Hollywood reporter

For in my mind, of all mankind
I love but you alone.

Anonymous, "The Nut Brown Maid"

7

ove seeketh not itself to please,
Nor for itself hath any care,
But for another gives its ease,
And builds a Heaven in Hell's despair.

William Blake, "Songs of Experience: The Clod and the Pebble"

SONNET #14

If thou must love me, let it be for nought
Except for love's sake only. Do not say
'I love her for her smile—her look—her way
Of speaking gently,—for a trick of thought
That falls in well with mine, and certes brought
A sense of pleasant ease on such a day'—
For these things in themselves, Beloved, may
Be changed, or change for thee,—and love so wrought,
May be unwrought so. Neither love me for
Thine own dear pity's wiping my cheeks dry,—
A creature might forget to weep, who bore
Thy comfort long, and lose thy love thereby!
But love me for love's sake, that evermore
Thou mayest love on, through love's eternity.

Elizabeth Barrett Browning

9

BELIEVE ME, IF ALL THOSE ENDEARING YOUNG CHARMS

Believe me, if all those endearing young charms
      Which I gaze on so fondly today,
Were to change by tomorrow, and fleet in my arms,
      Like fairy-gifts, fading away,
Thou would'st still be adored, as this moment thou art,
      Let thy loveliness fade as it will,
And around the dear ruin each wish of my heart
      Would entwine itself verdantly still.

It is not while beauty and youth are thine own,
      And thy cheeks unprofaned by a tear,
That the fervour and faith of a soul can be known,
      To which time will but make thee more dear;
No, the heart that has truly loved never forgets,
      But as truly loves on to the close,
As the sunflower turns on her god, when he sets,
      The same look which she turned when he rose.

Thomas Moore

I LOVE YOU AS NEW ENGLANDERS LOVE PIE!

Don Marquis, Sonnets to a Red-Haired Lady

LOVE CONSISTS IN THIS, THAT TWO SOLITUDES PROTECT
AND TOUCH AND GREET EACH OTHER.

Rainer Maria Rilke, Letters to a Young Poet

YOU'VE FALLEN INTO THE GREAT SEA OF LOVE
AND WITH YOUR PUNY SWIMMING WOULD ESCAPE!

Euripides, Hippolytus

I SHALL NOT BLUSH TO TELL YOU THAT YOU HAVE MADE
THE WHOLE WORLD BESIDES SO INDIFFERENT
TO ME THAT, IF I CANNOT BE YOURS, THEY MAY DISPOSE
OF ME AS THEY PLEASE.

Dorothy Osborne, in a letter to Sir William Temple

SONG: TO CELIA

Drink to me only with thine eyes,
And I will pledge with mine;
Or leave a kiss but on the cup,
And I'll not look for wine.
The thirst that from the soul doth rise,
Doth ask a drink divine:
But might I of Jove's nectar sup,
I would not change for thine.

I sent thee late a rosy wreath,
Not so much honoring thee,
As giving it a hope, that there
It could not withered be.
But thou thereon did'st only breathe,
And sent'st back to me;
Since when it grows and smells, I swear,
Not of itself, but thee.

Ben Jonson

Come live with me and be my love ...

MARRIAGE IS THE PERFECTION WHICH LOVE AIMED AT,
IGNORANT OF WHAT IT SOUGHT.

Ralph Waldo Emerson, Journals

SHE CAN EAT OUT OF MY SKILLET THE REST OF HER LIFE.

O. Henry, An Adjustment of Nature

TO SATISFY NATURE, THEN, A MAN NEED ONLY CHOOSE
A WOMAN WITH WHOM HE CAN DWELL IN TRANQUILITY
UNDER ONE ROOF ALL HIS LIFE.

Leon Battista Alberti, I Libri Della Famiglia

IT IS NOT GOOD THAT THE MAN SHOULD BE ALONE.

Genesis 11:18

The Passionate Shepherd to His Love

Come live with me and be my love,
And we will all the pleasures prove
That valleys, groves, hills, and fields,
Woods, or steepy mountain yields.

And we will sit upon the rocks,
Seeing the shepherds feed their flocks,
By shallow rivers to whose falls
Melodious birds sing madrigals.

And I will make thee beds of roses
And a thousand fragrant posies,
A cap of flowers, and a kirtle
Embroidered all with leaves of myrtle;

A gown made of the finest wool
Which from our pretty lambs we pull;
Fair lined slippers for the cold,
With buckles of the purest gold;

A belt of straw and ivy buds,
With coral clasps and amber studs:
And if these pleasures may thee move,
Come live with me and be my love.

The shepherds' swains shall dance and sing
For thy delight each May morning:
If these delights thy mind may move,
Come live with me and be my love.

Christopher Marlowe

Keep your eyes wide open
before marriage, half shut afterward.

Benjamin Franklin, Poor Richard's Almanac

Marriage remains practically inevitable; and the
sooner we acknowledge this, the sooner we shall set to
work to make it decent and reasonable.

Bernard Shaw, Getting Married

There is no such cozy combination
as a man and his wife.

Menander, The Principle Fragments, #647

LOVE SONNET BY A CIVIL SERVANT

Madam, I have the honour to submit,
Attached herewith, a schedule of your charms,
Register me, direct me, state me fit,
To hold that perfect form within my arms.
We are redundant in our single state,
Let our agreement be bilateral,
Let us our personnel co-ordinate
In passion mutual, reciprocal.
Let us resolve to frame a master plan,
For inter-departmental domicile
And add, as even civil servants can,
New Junior staff to our familial file,
I am, dear Madam (say it shall be so!)
Your most obedient servant. (1 Enclo.)
Dr. John D. Uytman.

Architect Christopher Wren's feathered namesakes are also architects, if not as famous for their designs. The English wren begins building a nest before he has a mate. Not satisfied, he abandons it and starts another one in a different site. Still not satisfied, he abandons the second and begins a third. Learning his trade by trial and error, the wren finally gets the nest right, and it is a thing of beauty. He builds it from spider's webs, grass, lichens, moss and hairs and lines the bottom with feathers. Then he puts a nice roof over the nest and makes a hole just big enough to fit through. Ready to settle down, the male ventures out, advertising his model home until he finds an interested female, whom he takes on an inspection trip to the site. Strutting ahead, he preens himself and coos sweet nothings as the female shyly follows behind, feigning indifference. At the site he shows her excitedly around the manse. If she likes what she sees, the deal is concluded and the two settle in for some serious billing and cooing.

Daniel Kaufman, Astonishing Facts About Animals

Animals That Mate for Life

Swans
Wolves
Eagles
Geese
Silverbacked Jackals
Cranes
Doves
Klipspringers
Marmosets
Ravens

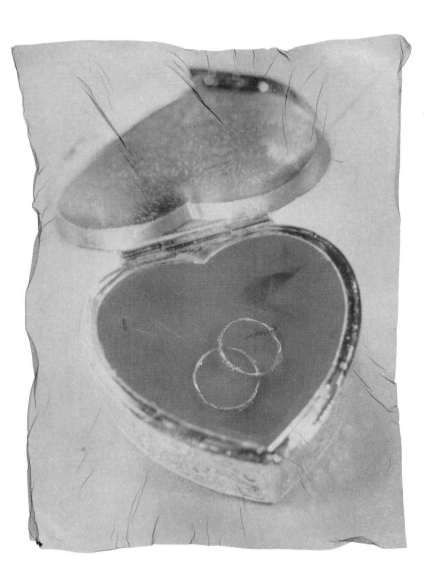

THE OWL AND THE PUSSY-CAT

1

The Owl and the Pussy-cat went to sea
    In a beautiful pea-green boat,
They took some honey, and plenty of money,
    Wrapped up in a five-pound note.
The Owl looked up to the stars above,
    And sang to a small guitar,
"O lovely Pussy! O Pussy, my love,
    What a beautiful Pussy you are,
        You are,
        You are!
    What a beautiful Pussy you are!"

2

Pussy said to the Owl, "You elegant fowl!
    How charmingly sweet you sing!
O let us be married! Too long have we tarried:
    But what shall we do for a ring?"
They sailed away, for a year and a day,
    To the land where the Bong-tree grows
And there in a wood, a Piggy-wig stood
    With a ring at the end of his nose,
        His nose,
        His nose,
    With a ring at the end of his nose.

3
"Dear Pig, are you willing to sell for one shilling
    Your ring?" Said the Piggy, "I will."
So they took it away, and were married next day
    By the Turkey who lives on the hill.
They dined on mince, and slices of quince,
    Which they ate with a runcible spoon;
And hand in hand, on the edge of the sand,
    They danced by the light of the moon,
        The moon,
        The moon,
    They danced by the light of the moon.

Edward Lear

With this ring . . .

The wedding ring is a traditional symbol of eternal love that dates back many centuries. Formed as a perfect circle, it has no beginning and no end. By some accounts, its historical meaning was somewhat less romantic—signifying the exchange of something of value for possession of the bride. In ancient Egypt, however, as well as more recently among the Anglo-Saxons, the ring seems to have symbolized the husband's trust that his wife would not abscond with his worldly wealth.

The widely practiced custom of wearing the ring on the fourth finger of the left hand arose from an ancient Roman belief that a nerve connected that finger directly to the heart. Later, the connection was said to be a vein, the *vena amoris*.

Even today, much solemn superstition surrounds the ring. Folk wisdom suggests the proper day of the week on which to buy it (never Friday) and how it should be handled (never let anyone try it on; never drop it during the ceremony). Among the mystical powers it supposedly boasts: a sliver of cake passed through it and then placed under the pillow of an unbetrothed young lady will bring dreams of a future husband.

A promise to love
(or, what was it I said?)

Marriage rests upon the immutable givens that compose it: words, bodies, characters, histories, places. Some wishes cannot succeed; some victories cannot be won; some loneliness is incorrigible. But there is relief and freedom in knowing what is real; these givens come to us out of the perennial reality of the world, like the terrain we live on. One does not care for this ground to make it a different place, or to make it perfect, but to make it inhabitable and to make it better. To flee from its realities is only to arrive at them unprepared.

Because the condition of marriage is worldly and its meaning communal, no one party to it can be solely in charge. What you alone think it ought to be, it is not going to be. Where you alone think you want it to go, it is not going to go. It is going where the two of you—and marriage, time, life, history, and the world—will take it. You do not know the road; you have committed your life to a way.

Wendell Berry, Standing by Words

To be your loving and faithful spouse in plenty and in want . . . in sickness and in health . . .

Presbyterian

To join with you and share all that is to come . . .

American Lutheran

To love and honor you all the days of my life . . .

Roman Catholic

In accordance with the laws of Moses and Israel . . .

Jewish

To laugh with you in joy;
to grieve with you in sorrow;
to grow with you in love;
serving mankind in peace and hope . . .

United Church of Canada

To recognize you as an equal individual, and always to be conscious of your development as well as my own. I shall seek through kindness and understanding to achieve with you the life we have envisioned . . .

Humanist

Let us share the joys.
We are word and meaning, united.
You are thought and I am sound.

Hindu

To have and to hold, from this day forward,
for better, for worse . . .
to love and cherish, till death do us part.

Traditional

Now you will feel no rain,
for each of you will be shelter for the other.
Now you will feel no cold,
for each of you will be warmth to the other.
Now there is no more loneliness.
Now you are two persons,
but there is only one life before you.
Go now to your dwelling to enter into
the days of your life together.
And may your days be good,
and long upon the earth.

Native American

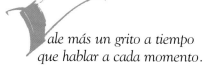

ale más un grito a tiempo
que hablar a cada momento.

Better one timely squawk than constant talk.

Jeff M. Sellers, Folk Wisdom of Mexico

Marriage has no enmities which
can survive a happy night.

Chinese Proverb

I pray you if you love me, bear my joy
A little while, or let me weep your tears;

. . .

Let us go forth together to the spring:
Love must be this, if it be anything.

Edna St. Vincent Millay, Collected Sonnets, "Sonnet #28"

35

Love well. Fight fair.

Love is a battle. Love is war. Love is growing up.

James Baldwin, quoted in the press after his death

Henry could be utterly insupportable; but he was always worth it. *Always!* And maybe, she paid me the compliment of adding, maybe when I got married, my wife would feel the same way about me. Insupportable, but worth it.

Aldous Huxley, The Genius and the Goddess

Have you ever read a modern American book on marriage or psychology which tells its readers to be quiet? The advice is always to talk out, feel out, or scream out your woes and they will go away. We're telling you to shut up.

William and Jane Appleton, How Not to Split Up

Alan and I have deep philosophical differences—not about religion, that's a snap—but about dustballs. He believes they are carriers of typhus and should be disposed of at once, preferably buried in a deep underground pit in Nevada.

I am convinced that dust balls are an act of God, not to be disturbed without filing an environmental impact statement.

Caryl Rivers, For Better, For Worse

Marriage is three parts love and seven parts forgiveness of sins.

Langdon Mitchell, The New York Idea

And baby makes three . . .

Of all those requirements, which particularly belong to the feminine character, there are none which take a higher rank, in our estimation, than such as enter into a knowledge of household duties; for on these are perpetually dependent the happiness, comfort, and well-being of a family. In this opinion we are borne out by the author of "The Vicar of Wakefield," who says: "The modest virgin, the prudent wife, and the careful matron, are much more serviceable in life than the petticoated philosophers, blustering heroines, or virago queens. She who makes her husband and her children happy, who reclaims the one from vice and trains up the other to virtue, is a much greater character than ladies described in romances, whose whole occupation is to murder mankind with shafts from their quiver, or their eyes."

Mrs. Isabella Beeton, Beeton's Book of Household Management
(originally published in 1859)

My wife and I were suddenly sharing the greatest moment in our lives. This was what we had asked God for; this was what we wanted to see if we could make. And I looked at it lovingly as they started to clean it off, but it wasn't getting any better.

And then I went over to my wife, kissed her gently on the lips, and said, "Darling, I love you very much. You just had a lizard."

Bill Cosby, Fatherhood

Why do fairy tales always end with the prince and princess marrying? Why don't they tell you what happened to the couple in the next fifty years? How did the prince and princess feel when the babies started coming? Did Cinderella ever wake up in the morning to the cry of her baby, feeling as evil and fussy as her stepsisters?

Angela Barron McBride, The Growth and Development of Mothers

The marriage that I write of in this book has nothing much to do with the lush, romantic visions of my youth. There are squirt guns, not fresh flowers, on my table. There are screams of "I'll tell Mom!", not strains of Bach. There is Diet Rite, not Beaujolais, at dinner. And the answer to "What's new?" is "The toilet seat broke."

Judith Viorst, Yes, Married

Who of us is mature enough for offspring before the offspring themselves arrive? The value of marriage is not that adults produce children, but that children produce adults.

Peter De Vries, The Tunnel of Love

Having kids is a pendulum of exuberance and pixilation, a ticktock of elation and droop. It leaves you breathless and confused. Why, it's almost like being in love.

Hugh O'Neill, Here's Looking at You, Kids

As long as you both shall live . . .

I ask not "Is thy heart still sure,
Thy love still warm, thy faith secure?"
I ask not "Dream'st thou still of me?"
Long'st always to fly to me?"
Ah, no—but as the sun includeth all
The good gifts of the Giver,
I sum all these in asking thee,
"Oh, sweetheart, how's your liver?"

Mark Twain, "A Love Song"

Married life. Is it worth it? Yes, it's worth it.
Yes it is. It's worth it because that man in my bed is
the man I still want to be there. It's worth it
because that man still makes me feel loved.

Judith Viorst, Yes, Married

One of the best things about love is
just recognizing a man's step when he
climbs the stairs.

Colette, Occupation

42

YOU MUST REMEMBER THIS,
A KISS IS STILL A KISS,
A SIGH IS JUST A SIGH;
THE FUNDAMENTAL THINGS APPLY,
AS TIME GOES BY.

Herman Hupfeld, "Everybody's Welcome (As Time Goes By)"

IN A SUCCESSFUL MARRIAGE THERE IS NO SUCH THING AS ONE'S WAY. THERE IS ONLY THE WAY OF BOTH, ONLY THE BUMPY, DUSTY, DIFFICULT, BUT ALWAYS MUTUAL PATH.

Phillis McGinley, The Province of the Heart

"NOTHING, SO IT SEEMS TO ME," SAID THE STRANGER, "IS MORE BEAUTIFUL THAN THE LOVE THAT HAS WEATHERED THE STORMS OF LIFE."

Jerome K. Jerome, The Passing of the Third Floor Back

Love seems the swiftest but it is the slowest of all growths. No man or woman really knows what perfect love is until they have been married a quarter of a century.

Mark Twain, Notebook

Thus hand in hand through life we'll go;
Its checkered paths of joy and woe
With cautious steps we'll tread.

Nathanial Cotton, "The Fireside"

The sweet, silent hours of marriage joys.

William Shakespeare, Richard III

The sun itself, which makes times, as they pass,
Is elder by a year, now, than it was
When thou and I first one another saw:
All other things to their destruction draw,
    Only our love hath no decay;
This, no tomorrow hath, or yesterday;
Running it never runs from us away,
But truly keeps his first, last, everlasting day.

John Donne, "The Anniversary"

We were together day and night for forty years and she never stopped amazing me.

George Burns, Gracie: A Love Story

FAMOUS COUPLES

Paul Newman & Joanne Woodward
George Burns & Gracie Allen
Cleopatra & Mark Anthony
Penelope & Odysseus
Popeye & Olive Oyl
Petrarch & Laura
Robin Hood & Maid Marian
Hume Cronyn & Jessica Tandy
Elizabeth Barrett & Robert Browning
Blondie & Dagwood
Edward VIII & Wallis Simpson
John & Abigail Adams
Tarzan & Jane
Roy Rogers & Dale Evans
Ozzie & Harriet

Romance exists in our marriage because we keep it there. Bob knows I care and I know he cares. We tell each other so and we guard our treasure carefully. We work hard to make sure nothing interferes with the lovely feelings we have for each other. We start each day with a hug and a kiss, and if there's something nice to be said, we say it.

Dorothy Greenwald, Learning to Live with the Love of Your Life

There is nothing nobler or more admirable than when two people who see eye to eye keep house, confounding their enemies and delighting their friends.

Homer, Odyssey

A good relationship has a pattern like a dance and is built on some of the same rules. The partners do not need to hold on tightly, because they move confidently in the same pattern, intricate but gay and swift and free, like a country dance of Mozart's. To touch heavily would be to arrest the pattern and freeze the movement, to check the endlessly changing beauty of its unfolding. There is no place here for the possessive clutch, the clinging arm, the heavy hand; only the barest touch in passing. Now arm in arm, now face to face, now back to back—it does not matter which. Because they know they are partners moving to the same rhythm, creating a pattern together, and being invisibly nurtured by it.

Anne Morrow Lindbergh, Gift from the Sea

Love me little, love me long
Is the burden of my song;
Love that is too hot and strong, burneth all to waste;
Still, I would not have thee cold,
Or backward or too bold,
For love that lasteth till 'tis old
Fadeth not in haste.

Anonymous

Sonnet #116

Let me not to the marriage of true minds
Admit impediments. Love is not love
Which alters when it alteration finds,
Or bends with the remover to remove:
Oh, no! It is an ever-fixéd mark,
That looks on tempests and is never shaken;
It is the star to every wandering bark,
Whose worth's unknown, although his height be taken.
Love's not Time's fool, though rosy lips and cheeks
Within his bending sickle's compass come;
Love alters not with his brief hours and weeks,
But bears it out even to the edge of doom.
If this be error and upon me proved,
I never writ, nor no man ever loved.

William Shakespeare

*G*row old along with me!
The best is yet to be.

Robert Browning, "Rabbi Ben Ezra"

Eve: If I ask myself why I love him, I find that I do not know, and do not really much care to know; so I suppose this kind of love is not a product of reasoning and statistics. . . . It just comes—none knows whence—and cannot explain itself. And doesn't need to.

. . .

Adam: Wheresoever she was, there was Eden.

Mark Twain, The Diary of Adam and Eve

Celebration . . .

REAFFIRMATION OF MARRIAGE VOWS

Some couples want to reaffirm their marriage vows on their twenty-fifth or fiftieth anniversaries. They may have—insofar as it is feasible—a duplicate of their wedding service if their church or synagogue and minister or rabbi agree. Many will not perform a "second" wedding ceremony but most will conduct a simple reaffirmation of vows.

In either case, as many members as possible of the original wedding party gather for the service. If it is permitted that a formal ceremony be held, then the best man and maid of honor are present, if possible, and they stand with the couple. If there are children from the marriage, they sometimes stand with the couple as well.

The "bride" should not wear her wedding dress, nor should the couple and attendants walk up the aisle. Women guests wear dresses appropriate to the hour of the day, and men wear business suits in the daytime and either suits or tuxedos, whichever is indicated, in the evening.

After the service, everyone may be invited to the couple's home for a reception, and a replica of the wedding cake may be served as dessert, or with coffee and champagne. Toasts by members of the "wedding party" and the couple's children are in order.

Elizabeth Post, Emily Post's Etiquette, *15th Edition*

Champagne Punch

3 RIPE PINEAPPLES

Cover pineapple and juice with:
1 LB. POWDERED SUGAR

Let mixture stand, covered, for 1 hour. Add:
2 CUPS LEMON JUICE
$^1/_2$ CUP CURAÇAO
$^1/_2$ CUP MARASCHINO LIQUEUR
2 CUPS BRANDY
2 CUPS LIGHT RUM

Stir and let stand for 4 hours. Place in a punch bowl with a block of ice.
Stir to blend and chill. Just before serving, add:

4 BOTTLES CHILLED CHAMPAGNE

Irma S. Rombauer and Marion Rombauer Becker, Joy of Cooking

FLOWERS TO MAKE AN ANNIVERSARY BOUQUET

Globe amaranth: Unfading love

Bluebell: Constancy

Dogwood: Durability

Forget-me-not: True love

Heliotrope: Devotion

Honeysuckle: Devoted affection

Ivy: Fidelity

Sweet pea: Lasting pleasures

China rose: Beauty always new

Red and white rose together: Unity

Red salvia: Forever thine

Stock: Lasting beauty

Veronica: Fidelity

Blue violet: Faithfulness

Kate Greenaway, The Language of Flowers

Acknowledgments

Two excerpts from "I pray you if you love me, bear my joy" by Edna St. Vincent Millay, from *Collected Poems,* Harper Collins, © 1922, 1923, 1950, 1951 by Edna St. Vincent Millay and Norma Millay Ellis. Reprinted by permission of Elizabeth Barnett, literary executor.

"Fragment #647" reprinted by permission of the publishers and Loeb Classical Library from *Menander: The Principle Fragments,* translated by Francis G. Allinson. Cambridge, MA: Harvard University Press, 1964.

Excerpt from *Folk Wisdom of Mexico* by Jeff M. Sellars, © 1994. Reprinted by permission of Chronicle Books, San Francisco.

Excerpt from *Learning to Live with the Love of Your Life* © 1970 by Robert and Dorothy Greenwald. Reprinted by permission of Harcourt Brace & Company.

Excerpt from *Sonnets to a Red-Haired Lady* by Don Marquis from *The Best of Don Marqui.* Reprinted by permission of Doubleday, a division of Bantam Doubleday Dell Publishing Group, Inc.

Excerpt from *Fatherhood* by Bill Cosby, © 1986 by William H. Cosby, Jr. Reprinted by permission of Bantam Books, a division of Bantam Doubleday Dell Publishing Group, Inc.

Excerpt from *Emily Post's Etiquette, 15th Edition* by Elizabeth L. Post, © 1992 by Elizabeth L. Post. Reprinted by permission of HarperCollins Publishers, Inc.

Excerpt from *How Not to Split Up,* © 1978 by Jane and William Appleton. Reprinted by permission of Doubleday, a division of Bantam Doubleday Dell Publishing Group, Inc.

Excerpt from *The Genius and the Goddess* by Aldous Huxley, © 1955 by Harper & Row. Reprinted by permission of The Estate of Aldous Huxley.

Excerpt from *Yes, Married* by Judith Viorst, © 1972. Reprinted by permission of The Saturday Review 1996, SR Publications, Ltd.

Excerpt from *A Humanist Wedding Service* by Corliss Lamont, pp. 7–8, © 1972, Buffalo, Prometheus Books. Reprinted by permission of the publisher.

Excerpt from "How to Get Along with Men" from *Province of the Heart* by Phyllis McGinley, © 1959 by Phyllis McGinley; renewed 1987 by Patricia Hayden Blake. Reprinted by permission of Viking Penguin, a division of Penguin Books USA Inc.

Excerpt from *Man and Superman* by Bernard Shaw. Reprinted by permission of The Society of Authors on behalf of the Bernard Shaw Estate.

Excerpt from *Joy of Cooking* by Irma Rombauer and Marion Rombauer Becker, © 1931, 1936, 1941, 1943, 1946, 1951, 1952, 1953, 1962, 1963, 1964, 1975 by Bobbs-Merrill. Reprinted by permission of Simon & Schuster.

Excerpt from *Gift from the Sea* by Anne Morrow Lindbergh, © 1955. Reprinted by permission of Pantheon Books, a Division of Random House, Inc.

Excerpt from *I Libri Della Famiglia* by Leon Battista Alberti, translated by Renee N. Watkins. Reprinted by permission of Renee N. Watkins.